ROCK BOTTOM

Copyright @ 2024 by Shannon Maier

Photographer: Bailey L. Williams

This book is dedicated to:
You
For all the sleepless nights and endless days of despair that you have endured since the bottom fell out.

Joshua 1:9
"Be strong and courageous. Do not be afraid; do not be discouraged, for the Lord your God will be with you wherever you go"

And to my loving family, Scott, Brooke & Bailey whom God personally placed around me on my darkest days to be forever what He knew I needed most..*unconditional love*

Table of Contents

FORWARD

To my soul crushed friend;

If you are holding this book in your hands, I know that you are most likely at the deepest part of a pit or canyon you have ever been in. You have hit Rock Bottom!

You have hit hard and the pain is unbearable. Beloved, your cry does not fall to the bleak dark of night, nor are your tears left to dry without stain or purpose. The fallout has not been without great anguish and distress.

Your thoughts may be something like this, " With no relief in sight, it would be easier to be eaten by the fowl of the air, rather than to try to make any effort to get myself up and out of this God forsaken hole that I am in, at this moment in time."

With today being the first day of the rest of your life it very likely would be your last if it was up to you.
 Your mind is a black cloud of confusion and chaos. Your circumstances have taken your breath away. Your outlook is beyond bleak and your pain is beyond trying to make sense of the next few days, let alone the approaching hours.

The word *"hope"* is long sought after in times like this, but even scripture reminds us, when hope is deferred, it makes the body sick. When all hope is lost it disappears like the shadows on a rainy day. No ray of sunshine, no light in the dark, and definitely no hope for a brighter tomorrow.

Although these words sound wearily familiar from where you sit or lie today, could I please offer you a rope. A rope of *HOPE*.

I have written this book as a declaration of hope to all who have hit ROCK BOTTOM and need to be rescued.

I realize there could only be one word that would make any sense for someone in your shoes. Lord knows you don't need any more advice, and you certainly don't need a new way of thinking, you simply need someone to *rescue* you!

If there was a lifeline of hope for you and all that afflicts you in this hour, would you reach for it? I want you to know that it will not take any effort on your part, as I know there is nothing left in you to give. It is simply your "yes" to an invitation to someone who will run to your *rescue*.

There is a person who would love to save you and wants nothing more than to *rescue* you, no matter how far you have fallen. Regardless if it was due to your own misstep or that of another. There is a rescue team coming and His name is Jesus. That was and is His sole mission. To save and rescue us.

Some may say, I already know Him and really am questioning how he let me fall this far in the first place. For others, this may be the first time in your life that you have ever considered calling on His name, because you've tried everything, and nothing else has turned out. So, this is your last ditch effort, to be saved. Either way, He is on his way.

Look up *HOPE* is here to stay.

Please take this book as slow as you need to go. It is short for a reason. I know you barely have enough in you to sleep or eat, let alone try to comprehend tiny black words on the following pages. One thing I do know. I have been in the exact place that you are. And I didn't need another self help book. I needed someone to rescue me from this pit that I found myself in.

There is no rush or race. Jesus wants to heal you everywhere you hurt. As with every great physician, it takes precise timing and surgical tools to restore the body when it has been broken. The same is true for you, friend.

Allow the pages ahead to feel like a blanket of comfort wrapped around you. I pray that the words will become life giving to you as the air that you need to breathe. Let each word be the breath of life that will sustain you when you are not sure that you can go any further.

When you are parched, let pages serve as living water on the days when you walk through the most dry and thirsty land. Especially on the days you beg for relief.

I know you are tired and ready to give in. But walk with me a little farther and you will see that the Lord is good!

Are you ready? Look up beloved, your rescue team is on their way down now. It won't be long and you will be safe in the arms of JESUS. Take his hand, you can trust Him, I promise.

I will see you at the top…

Rock Climbing Verse:

Psalm 86:13 TPT You love me so much, and you have placed your greatness upon me. You rescued me from the deepest place of darkness, and you have delivered me from a certain death.

CRIES FROM THE CANYON

Psalm 102: 6 & 7

"Hear my prayer, O Lord; listen to my cry for mercy. In the day of my trouble I will call to you, for you will answer me."

Lying at the bottom of the deepest darkest part of the canyon, where you once looked with astonishment from above, you now lie flat on your back with every part of your being, broken and possibly even shattered into a million pieces. You find yourself in a helpless state of both hysteria and disbelief, realizing this is *now your* life! When just a few short moments ago you were on top of the world, literally. With one step you find yourself brought down to nothing... a mere inexistence of this universe. "How did it happen?" How can this be?" What should I have done differently?" If only I would have been more cautious?! If only I could have seen it coming?" All are the questions that we have asked ourselves over and over when the bottom somehow inexplicably falls out.

You cry for help, but tears that come with your voice fall to the bleak coldness of the rocks that have broken your fall. No one in sight or sound of your impaired voice for miles and miles. You feel as if you have been left to die.

In and out of consciousness you realize that you *will* live, but recognize that death would be much more painless. Apprehensive at what the future holds, you can't move. Seconds go by like a day in a cold, dark and dreary snow storm that lasts for weeks. A time when the sun never seems to shine. Depression and despair set in all around you. The situation is bigger than life, and you come to realize that life as you once knew it, is *now* gone, forever!

Unlike literally being at the bottom of the canyon, to be eaten alive by the fowl of the air, you realize that you are lying face down on the floor of your own living room, the corner of your bedroom, or wherever life has handed you this deck of cards when you collapsed. You realize that you will have to get up by yourself and face the world and all that it holds... only to look at the repulsive demon in the face that has brought you to your knees to be knocked back down to size every time you realize that this is not a dream, this is *your* reality.

Maybe it is an unplanned pregnancy for your teenage daughter. A husband who has left you to raise your children on your own, while he finds someone else to occupy his time. Possibly it is a blood test that has confirmed that you have a life altering disease. Knowing just a few days ago you were only being a good citizen and giving blood to the betterment of mankind. Possibly, you have been diagnosed with terminal cancer that has dictated your years into days.

How can this be? How can *any* of this be? Everything was fine just a few short minutes ago...

By now your own story is ringing louder than ever...we all have one, you know?! Where do you turn when all else is gone? When all of your options are exhausted? When there are **no** options at all? There is nothing left to do, but survive. To breathe in and breathe out. You stare desperately into the darkness of space, where it feels like you have been frozen in time, while the rest of the world passes you by. The place you can feel the beat of every blood vessel that pumps through your veins faster and faster with each passing second.

You wonder who will hear your cries? Who will come to your rescue? Who will awaken you from this nightmare? Who will stop the pain and suffering, the sleepiness nights, and the cold drenched sheets from your endless tears?

Who can it be? Is there anybody out there?!

Most generally, we look to ourselves for short-term fixes, like sex, drugs, alcohol, shopping, gambling, social media, compulsive behavior and even denial. We often say, "this really isn't happening." And then we begin to drown ourselves in the numbness of life. These are the perfect distractions that the enemy so deliberately and skillfully hands us on a silver platter. Relentless, he persuades you to give in to his bidding and leaves you for dead.

Many times we talk ourselves into something like this, "If I can just keep myself occupied with my surroundings, then possibly it will fade away." But as you and I both know, that is never the case. That is a momentary easement. You still have to wake up to the crippling circumstances at hand, and realize at the break of dawn that this was NOT a dream, this is the truth!

Crying out in the dark of night, to the emptiness of the black air, brings almost the same level of pain that you experience with the first initial blow of knowing that life will never be the same. The feeling of helplessness and hopelessness are indescribable. The desperation of handling it all on your own is more than any human being can endure. How in the world do you make sense of it all?

Finding the answers to these primary questions after the fall is key to finding the escape hatch to come up and out.

No matter what hand you have been dealt, knowing that you never have to handle it alone, is the first part of this passage. Realizing that you will always have someone beside you when the road gets even tougher will give you the hope you will need to continue on your journey. There will be someone to hold your right hand, to carry you through the flames of life when the fire is so intense, you can feel your surroundings melt away. Someone to hold your head above the waters so you are not swept away by the raging river of circumstance that carries everything of value downstream. Someone to block the fiery darts that are continually shot in your direction, aiming straight toward your already bleeding heart.

Is there really someone like this to help me? Is there really a knight and shining armor, a warrior, a guardian angel, perhaps a king? Yes! Actually the one coming to your rescue is the King of all Kings...someone more powerful than the sun that lights the day. A man who has more strength than the thunder and lightning by night. . Who is this person, where in the world can I find him? I know I have read about him in the scriptures. But is this Jesus really real?

If so, I appeal to Him at once. I am truly at his mercy.

God tells us in His word, "Come all of you who are weary and heavy burdened and I will give you rest. In Matthew 11:28. Jesus is appealing to us all, not the other way around. He first makes the invitation on our behalf. Somehow that has got to be an encouragement to those of us who are at the end of their rope.

I want to remind you, He doesn't say, "all of you that have made the right decisions, done all the right things, *then* I will come and help you." No, He says, "Come ALL of you who are weary and heavily burdened and I will take care of you." No questions asked.

Unfortunately, many of us think that is the only way that God will help us. If we earn it, then He will take care of us. Just like our earthly father would check our chore chart to see if we had completed all of our duties before he would reward us. That is quite the contrary. He loves us so much that no matter what we do His love will never change. Believe it or not, we could make a lifetime of bad decisions, and He would still be there for us to come and rescue us.

I too have landed in the deepest darkest pit that I never want to remember. In my journey, I often asked if God had caused it. Not necessarily, but I do believe He allowed me to be there a while for His divine reason and His heavenly intervention. Are the pits that I have fallen into because I chose to get off track into dangerous territory? Unfortunately, yes! At times, did Satan lay and wait for me and set a trap for me to fall into? Absolutely yes! Did God say, "Ok, this is not what I want for you, but I will allow it to draw you closer to rely on me, a resounding, YES!"

You see, there comes a time when you are all out of options but to cry. To wail beyond comprehendible words, when you are at the end of all rational emotions. The cries from the canyon are the most excruciating tears that you will ever feel run down your face. They are the outward moaning and gut-wrenching pain that has you feeling like Jesus did in the Garden of Gethsemane.

Where do your tears of pain fall? What do they feel like? Are they wasted in a room that is darkened with demons and evil spirits that taunt you? Or are they seen by a gracious and loving Father that comes to the rescue of his child that is fragile and broken?

He is the Father that races to catch the tears in a bottle (Ps. 56:8) then later records them in His journal for safe keeping so he can track every droplet as if they were of precious wine or perfume. That is what Jesus says about your tears. They are the water from the well of your soul. And if Jesus died to save your soul, why would he not want to save what flows from it?

The Psalms are filled with verses that state when David cried out, God came running. Running to his rescue. Running to pick him up, and to place him under his wings or to hide him in the cleft of a rock from the enemy and even to wipe his tears. *(For an awesome bible study, read where there are 31 times in Psalms alone where the Psalmists cries out and God replies)*

There is a key factor in crying out to God…Cry out loud! How many times have you cried inwardly and kept the pain enclosed so no one could hear or see you? Then ask yourself, how many times have you cried out loud in an audible voice that could be heard? The numbers are far and few between, I am sure.

There is something very humbling about saying the words out loud for God to hear. Yes, He already knows your heart, but what does it do to you? For you to hear it and then for the enemy to hear your cries to the Father. If you want to move the heart of God, cry out to him with the sound of your voice. He is waiting to hear from you. I know at first it may seem awkward and sometimes even childlike, but I guarantee He hears you and He comes to comfort you in your hour of need. Remember, Jesus asks us to come like children. So come! Come and cry at the feet of Jesus.

You may find peace that you have never experienced before. You may suddenly feel joy in your heart again. You may get a clear mind that will allow you to think reasonably for the first time in a long time. A whole host of events can come from a single cry from the canyon. It may be the words and tears that are needed to begin your journey to freedom. To a higher place. To a resting place. To the place of total healing.

What could your tears be holding back? What victory could come your way, by simply shedding a tear of two, or a hundred and two?

Throughout the bible, many people cried out in their sadness. Jesus cried over the death of his friend Lazarus. Mary cried at the foot of the cross. David cried over his sin toward God when he committed adultery with Bathsheba, along with many others.

I believe it is a very significant part of the bible that God uses to show us his genuine love in our time of despair. Have you ever wondered what He would do if you would allow Him into the most vulnerable places in your heart?

Why don't you take the time and share your heart with Him? He will be by your side when you do.

ROCK CLIMBING NOTES:

If you now find yourself on the edge of a cliff, at the bottom of a pit, or in the corner of your bedroom holding back the tears, can I encourage you to let them go? Release them and allow God to place them in a sacred bottle just for you. They are precious to Him, and He wants to heal you everywhere you hurt. He wants to touch your heart like no one has ever touched you.

If there is just one thing you can do today, take a moment and cry out to God. Get alone, get in your car, go to the basement, climb a tree, wherever you can go, get away with Him just for a moment and cry out the words that are so heavy on your heart.

Tell Him you can't make it on your own, and you don't want to go any farther without Him. There is nothing special or fancy about crying out to God. It is just you and Him. He will not tell a soul, I promise. Your secrets are safe. He loves you dear friend. He has brought you to this exact moment in time to call upon Him, so that He can save you from your sorrow. Will you trust Him with those precious tears? Just try Him and see…see what tomorrow will bring, I think you will be amazed!!!

BROKENNESS

Psalm 147:3
"He heals the brokenhearted and binds up their wounds"

The descent was damaging, the fall gut wrenching and the pain is beyond any words that could ever be expressed in your entire lifetime.

Landing deep in the ravine of brokenness, you begin to feel every fractured part of your body. Not only have your fingers and toes grown numb from the severing from life to limb, but you also are reeling in and out of consciousness from such pain and agony in your mind.

Lying here in this darkened place of disbelief and complete bewilderment, it would be much easier to lay here and die then to get up and begin to take a step to locate help to rescue your soul. (Or at least that is what the enemy would have you believe.)

Our arms and legs can easily be set in a cast to heal. However, what happens when you can't see the fragmented pieces through an x-ray machine, no less handle the full intensity of its pain from your circumstance?

In a day and age where simple flaws and freckles are automatically filtered through our phone screens, a broken smile or a fractured spirit would be unheard of to consider sharing with a friend or family member, let alone a post on social media.

We often hide our brokenness with fake smiles and even more fraudulent lives. We play our highlight reels like it is our normal everyday life, while we are literally dying inside. The world has put on the biggest act that the stage has ever seen. Many of us are truly dying while believing that someone else has it all together.

We have learned to cover up our pain with sports and surprise parties. We camouflage our pain with pills and plenty of places to go. If only we could keep this pace, then we would never have to stop long enough to feel the pain. Our world has become experts at anesthetizing the pain that tortures us day and night while leaving us completely shattered on the inside.

Although no one ever signs up for brokenness, this can be one of the most valuable experiences of our lifetime. Psalm 34:18 says, *The Lord is near to the brokenhearted and saves those who are crushed in spirit.*

Have you felt crushed or broken recently? Believe it or not, this is good news for you, because Jesus has never been closer. If we would learn to embrace our brokenness instead of our independence we might realize we are in the best place possible.
Jesus never wants us or asks us to go it alone. He wants us to stay so close to him so that nothing can come in between us.

I know when I am broken and unable to breathe, I rarely look for safety. I simply just want to fall down and die. I feel as though I can't move another inch. So wherever life handed me this blow, I want to quit! But Jesus says it differently. He says, "let me hold you, let me envelop you, protect you and cover you."

He wants nothing more than to make Himself your dwelling place. Even when I feel deeply alone, I must remind myself that I am never alone.

It was in my darkest hours that the Lord revealed something so profound that I will never forget or fear the darkened places again. He showed me through His word in Psalm 91, that when He tucks me up under his wing, then I am the absolute closest that I can be to Him. That also means that more than likely that he has led me to a place with very little light. It was the scheme of Satan that led me to believe that God had left me alone in those dark places. That was not true at all. The truth of the matter is that I am by far the closest to Him when I can't even see my hand in front of my face. And this my friend is called, " The shelter of the Most High"

My prayer is that this gives you a new found hope where you can find safety. Right next to Jesus.

Unfortunately, we get so far ahead of God and fall into situations that we may be experiencing right now. But not everyone's circumstances are due to their poor decisions. However, there are many of us suffering today because we thought we knew best and went out of our safe confines and away from Christ.

Regardless if it was your doing or from another, God isn't focused on who's fault it is, He is more interested in taking what is broken and making it brand new. He wants to take you to safety.

Friend, no matter how many pieces you may be in, God is right there with you. He will never leave you or forsake you. You are not alone!

Rock Climbing Verse:

Psalm 91:1-6 says, " Whoever dwells in the shelter of the Most High will rest in the shadow of the Almighty. I will say of the Lord, "He is my refuge and my fortress, my God, in whom I trust." Surely he will save you from the fowler's snare and from the deadly pestilence. He will cover you with his feathers, and under his wings you will find refuge; his faithfulness will be your shield and rampart. You will not fear the terror of night, nor the arrow that flies by day, nor the pestilence that stalks in the darkness, nor the plague that destroys at midday."

DEATH WITHOUT THE COFFIN

Death-Wikiquote:

Death is the permanent end of the life of a biological organism. Death may refer to the end of life as either an event or condition.

The last time I checked, the death rate was hovering around 100%. We are all going to die. Encouraging? Not really! But we do have hope.

Deuteronomy. 30:11-15 *"Now what I am commanding you today is not too difficult for you or beyond your reach. It is not up in heaven, so that you have to ask, who will ascend into heaven to get it and proclaim it to us so we may obey it? Nor is it beyond the sea, so that you have to ask, "Who will cross the sea to get it and proclaim it to us so we may obey it? No, the word is very near you; it is in your mouth and in your heart so that you may obey it. See, I set before you today life and prosperity, death and destruction. Choose life."*

No matter what happens to the rest of the world, there will always be Life and Death.

No matter if a baby was conceived and did not make it out of the mothers womb alive or you live to the ripe old age of 120, we all will face certain death.

Death is natural, sometimes grotesque and grueling. Other times it is peaceful and promising. Either way, none of us can avoid it.

Despite your age, nearly all of us have attended a funeral, a mass, awake, or a celebration of life.

Regardless if they were a close family member, a distant friend or acquaintance, most of us have passed by the coffin or urn where someone has been laid to rest..

The coffin or casket, the box or tomb no matter what you call it; all share a similarity. It is someone's final resting place. Their finality, their conclusion, or their inevitability. We all will face it at some point in time. Some of us sooner than later. No one ever knows the day. Only God holds the privilege of knowing when our life here on earth will be over.

But what about the death of those things that don't require a coffin or an urn? No ceremony or ritual.

A dying marriage? A dead relationship? A lifeless dream? Or a departed opportunity? A life altering disease that cripples you or your loved one for the remainder of your lives.

It's a death without a memorial service. No calling hours or visitation to mourn the loss of your beloved. No flowers or sympathy cards, no hugs or holding of your hands. Just pain and sorrow from your aching heart.

I have attended more of these services than I ever would want to recall. The sad part about it, I attended them alone.

There was no reception line. No one dressed up in their Sunday black best, and there were certainly not any fragrant blossoms or wind chimes that hung in the shadows.

No, it was more like me, myself and I. No loving grandmother to pat my hand. No parents to hold on to, and no spouse to hide behind to make the nightmare seem to be less frightening.

I have found, the longer I travel on this journey called life, I am met many times over with the reoccurrence of another passing.

Recently it has been the passing of my husband. Not in literal form, but in the figurative. Well, honestly it is both. It has been 7 years now since the diagnosis of his stage 4 renal cell carcinoma.

A 15 cm tumor (the size of a football) including his kidney, lymph nodes and adrenal gland had been removed to rid his body of as much cancer as they could.

As with stage 4 cancer patients, their prognosis is often grim. They rarely don't do any more surgeries after the initial one. They are most likely filled up with chemo or radiation, then told to hope for the best and to prepare for the worst.

In our case, chemo and radiation did not affect this type of cancer, so we had to look toward other alternatives to keep any new cancers away.

Treatment started and stopped. Off and on for the following two years. He often became too sick to handle any more medicine. His symptoms were so severe at times that he would have to rest and wait so we could try again.

All in all, these last 84 months have been grueling to say the least.

As I write this book, he is currently in hospice. Not because of the cancer, but because of what the cancer treatments did to his body.

Anyone who has had cancer or is a close caregiver of a cancer patient or a terminal disease knows all too well that the day-to-day exhaustion will become your constant companion.

Simple everyday chores become a monumental endeavor. Three loads of laundry look like Mt Everest. Sweeping and mopping the floors seems like you have been asked to scrub the city streets with a toothbrush. And the grocery store, well, you might as well be asked to press your way through Time Square on New Year's Eve while pushing your cart and acquiring the necessities for a few days of survival.

There are no small tasks any more. Taking a shower can be a colossal event. Washing all your 2000 parts becomes more than you have the strength to muster.

These days have become my constant. Getting up and putting on make-up on and driving to work is the start of an enormous struggle.

Within nine short minutes of departing my home and entering reality, while I leave my husband behind to suffer in the confines of the cancer chaos, I find that I am uncontrollably inept to go throughout my day without some form of breakdown.

It's only because I see death all around me. I am awakened in the middle of the night with my husband gasping for air through his oxygen tank. I see death in my dreams as I stand over my own open pit of bereavement and grip my toes in fear that I too will fall to my sure and sudden death.

I see death when I awaken and look into his eyes as they are glazed with yellow from a toxic liver that is being attacked from the medicine that is ultimately supposed to spare his life if he is lucky.

I see death as I arrive at school from students who have attempted suicide the night before or have cut marks on their forearms to release their own pain of death from within their own teenage years of despair.

I see death through my associates of lost souls and their helpless and hopeless way of life. I hear death pouring out of the mouths of both adults and children as every word that comes off their tongue brings sure and sudden death to their mind, bodies and spirits.

I see the death of my dreams as I yearn to make something great with my own life, and yet all that really gets accomplished are buying more Kleenex boxes and purchasing even more prescriptions to keep my husband alive and our family together.

Death is imminent! I can see it, taste it and smell it. I know what death looks like. It follows me. But does it have to swallow me up every single day of my life? God is showing me it doesn't have to.

I began to believe at times, death was more prominent than living. There were no more happy days, and joy filled hours. Now, there were just tear filled pillow cases, and empty medicine bottles. They all entered our home with the reality that death is very present. And that I would have to attend a funeral nearly every day of my life.

Lately, I have found myself standing over an open grave more than I wanted to. Figurative funerals were my constant. I found I was running out of black clothing due to all the

services. But in actuality there was no body to speak of.
Only devastating dreams, perishing promises and terrible
tragedies.

Daily visits to any morgue or cemetery for anyone would be
unhealthy. But what happens when you must visit monthly,
weekly or even daily without your consent?

What happens when death stares you down in the face in the
mirror, in your spouse, in your checkbook, or in your family
unit? What happens when you not only see death in your
circumstance but where you *can* taste it, *smell* it, and *even feel*
it.

The breath of death creeping down your spine can be the most
chilling feeling of all. There is no escape from its stench and
its heavy hollow pants can scare the daylights out of even the
toughest of men and women.

As I wrestle with it day after day and night after night, I have
come to realize these death stares will not be my first nor my
last?

Death is what keeps us humble and life in perspective. Life is
fragile. We must never take it for granted, as we are never
promised tomorrow.

The only hope I can find is that it does not have to overtake
us. Jesus said, I have come to conquer death so that we may
live, and live to the full!

Maybe your days, months and years have looked more like a
constant funeral procession like mine. I get it! Believe me, I
really get it. But could I encourage you today, to step away for
just a moment from the coffin? The grave? The very casket

that most likely holds all of your hopes and dreams and lean into these words…

Deut. 30: 19; *"This day I call the heavens and the earth as witnesses against you that I have set before you life and death, blessings and curses. Now choose life, so that you and your children may live."*

Every single day of our numbered lives we are given a choice. An opportunity to choose life or death. It is that simple. I didn't say it was easy, but it is that simple.

God has not promised us a rose covered pathway toward our eternal home, but He does promise us a safe landing.

There will be many opportunities to live or die along the way. Regardless of the circumstances that you are presently facing. The choice is up to you.

Just as I had to make the decision every day to put both feet on the floor and breathe in the air that God had provided, I knew I had to choose to live even when every part of my body said to just lay down and die. I knew I had to keep going with everything that was in me, even if there wasn't much left at all.

I Corinthians 12:10, encourages me, that when I am weak, He is strong. So, the less of me, the more of Christ I get.

'That is why, for Christ's sake, I delight in weaknesses, insults, in hardships, in persecutions, in difficulties. For when I am weak, then I am strong.'

Christ came that we might have life and have it to the full. But it took His death on the cross for us to obtain this life. It is here that I began to understand the way of death more clearly.

God asks us to die to ourselves daily. You see, death isn't always a depraved entity as I used to think. Because when something is put to death, a resurrected life can come from it.

When a dead seed is placed in the dark shallows of the earth, it can be brought back to life to produce more life.

Jesus was the same. He had to be crucified on the cross and laid in the tomb, so that we could live with Him eternal. His death made it possible for us to live forever and not to experience a permanent death.

Unfortunately, it has taken my husband's cancer to heal me from more things than I would like to admit. The things that needed to be put to rest in my own soul. It was the raw experiences through his suffering that stripped me of myself.

My need to have everything in order was simply my need to be in control. That needed to die long ago. My need to know and plan every detail of my life was something that made me absolutely crazy mentally and physically which meant I needed to start digging.

My need to have my own way so life could follow suit as I deemed it necessary, was not the life of sacrifice that Christ had called me too. God said, that must go too.

Putting to death my "people pleasing" habit was a funeral that I have attended more than once and probably will be many more times than I'd like to admit.

All and all the constant procession of funerals of self was something that I have grown accustomed to. I am beginning to feel like the funeral director preparing a body for the 1000th time.

Somehow in God's sovereignty my overwhelming emotions are dying. The stench of death isn't so overwhelming and I now know how to handle the hurst when it pulls in front of my house. All the dead body parts are simply tools in God's hands to make me new.

If God sees something in my life and says, "that's got to go", I might as well begin digging myself, because I know what soon follows.

The hole, the heartache, the helpless feeling, and then the healing. Thank God for the healing!

Just like for some cancer patients who are not healed on this side of heaven, they soon will be made well after their bodies leave this earth. For those of us left behind, we feel the sting of death, but for them, they only feel and see the glory of heaven.

Death is no longer in their future; they are finally made whole and begin to live life to the fullest. And honestly, that is what we all look forward to, isn't it?

Regardless of where you stand today, whether that is a literal or figurative graveside, let me assure you that you do not stand alone.

Jesus too was saddened by death. He knows our pain. His close friend Lazarus lay dead four days before he stood by his graveside. But it was there that Jesus also called him out of the grave to live again.

Maybe you feel like me and are tired of lying in the dirt for the worms to crawl between your toes. You're tired of being a ditch dweller. Friend, Jesus calls you up and out of the grave. To shake off those grave clothes and to live again. The way He had intended.

Read this amazing passage in Ezekiel 37 and see if you don't hear God calling you to prophesy to your own dry bones and to live again!

"The LORD took hold of me, and I was carried away by the Spirit of the LORD to a valley filled with bones. ² He led me all around among the bones that covered the valley floor. They were scattered everywhere across the ground and were completely dried out. ³ Then he asked me, "Son of man, can these bones become living people again?"

"O Sovereign LORD," I replied, "you alone know the answer to that."

⁴ Then he said to me, "Speak a prophetic message to these bones and say, 'Dry bones, listen to the word of the LORD! ⁵ This is what the Sovereign LORD says: Look! I am going to put breath into you and make you live again! ⁶ I will put flesh and muscles on you and cover you with skin. I will put breath into you, and you will come to life. Then you will know that I am the LORD.'"

⁷ So I spoke this message, just as he told me. Suddenly as I spoke, there was a rattling noise all across the valley. The bones of each body came together and attached themselves as complete skeletons. ⁸ Then as I watched, muscles and flesh formed over the bones. Then skin formed to cover their bodies, but they still had no breath in them. ⁹ Then he said to me, "Speak a prophetic message to the winds, son of man. Speak a prophetic message and say, 'This is what the

Sovereign LORD says: Come, O breath, from the four winds!
Breathe into these dead bodies so they may live again.'"

[10] So I spoke the message as he commanded me, and breath
came into their bodies. They all came to life and stood up on
their feet—a great army.

[11] Then he said to me, "Son of man, these bones represent the
people of Israel. They are saying, 'We have become old, dry
bones—all hope is gone. Our nation is finished.' [12] Therefore,
prophesy to them and say, 'This is what the Sovereign LORD
says: O my people, I will open your graves of exile and cause
you to rise again. Then I will bring you back to the land of
Israel. [13] When this happens, O my people, you will know that
I am the LORD. [14] I will put my Spirit in you, and you will live
again and return home to your own land. Then you will know
that I, the LORD, have spoken, and I have done what I said.
Yes, the LORD has spoken!'"

Can you imagine what this must have looked like? For dry
bones to come alive literally? Maybe you too feel like this
vast field of brokenness. And you need the Living God to
breathe life again in your mind, your body and your spirit.
You may need a fresh wind for your family, your finances and
your friendships. No matter what it may be, ask the Lord to
resurrect what has expired.

God is a God of miracles. And the last time I checked He was
doing them every day. So, no matter how bleak your situation
may look today, can I encourage you to trust in the Lord who
can and does say, "rise up and walk", so you can live again!

Survival Guide Note:

Remember this, while we are still here in our earthly bodies, we live in a fallen world. God will continue to ask us to pick up our cross and die to our self-daily, but it is not for a lost cause. It is merely so that we can live the life that He died to give us to the full.

I don't know that I will ever grow accustomed to death or the loss that comes from it, but I do know that on the other side is a beautiful place called Glory. The Promised Land. For those of us in Christ, we will no longer witness death ever again. Wow, what a day that will be!

So, rejoice and take heart in the fact that whatever is dead in your life can and will be made brand new if you allow God to do what He does best. Restore-Redeem-Resurrect!

He may be asking you to take part in the matter. He may ask you to bury what is lost. He may ask you to dig and plant what seems to show no growth. He may ask you to climb up on the cross for your own crucifixion. He may even ask you to keep giving of yourself when you simply want to lay down and die. Regardless of what He asks of you, our job is simply to trust and obey for there really is no other way. Peace be with you friend as you lay it to rest.

Your Savior stands right next to you at the side of this grave. He too will call you to "come out and live again" just like he did his friend Lazarus.

ROCK CLIMBING Verses:

John 11:17-26

On his arrival, Jesus found that Lazarus had already been in the tomb for four days. Now Bethany was less than two miles from Jerusalem, and many Jews had come to Martha and Mary to comfort them in the loss of their brother. When Martha heard that Jesus was coming, she went out to meet him, but Mary stayed at home. "Lord," Martha said to Jesus, "if you had been here, my brother would not have died. But I know that even now God will give you whatever you ask." Jesus said to her, "Your brother will rise again." Martha answered, "I know he will rise again in the resurrection at the last day." Jesus said to her, "I am the resurrection and the life. The one who believes in me will live, even though they die; and whoever lives by believing in me will never die. Do you believe this?"

I Corinthians 15:55-58

Where, O death, is your victory? Where, O death, is your sting?" " The sting of death is sin, and the power of sin is the law. But thanks be to God! He gives us the victory through our Lord Jesus Christ. Therefore, my dear brothers and sisters, stand firm. Let nothing move you. Always give yourselves fully to the work of the Lord, because you know that your labor in the Lord is not in vain.

DELIVERANCE

"Psalms 34:4 I sought the LORD, and he answered me; he delivered me from all of my fears"

In a day in age where anything and everything can be delivered to your front door in an instant, why is it so difficult for us to have the same delivery service from our fears, sins, pain and suffering?

What would it feel like to pull up an app, make a selection and tap "place your order" and send it into the heavens and soon experience a delivery service like never before?

There it is in your cart… Free from addiction. Free from anger. Free from jealousy. Free from insecurity. Free from sickness. Free from fear of the unknown. Completely free from whatever ails you and delivered to your door in an instant!

Wow! Sign me up!

Wouldn't it be amazing if it were that simple?

Believe it or not, it can be. But the truth of the matter is, that there is work to be done first. Now, before you sigh a big huge "ugh", let me reassure you that this work doesn't fall on you as much as it does Jesus.

All throughout the scriptures, we see men, women and children being delivered from some form of bondage in their lives. Whether that was the issue of blood, or from demons, or even years of being paralyzed. There is nothing Jesus doesn't wish to deliver us from. That's why He came to earth. To set us FREE!

I love the definition in Webster's Dictionary. DELIVERANCE: the act of delivering someone or something. {Especially: LIBERATION, RESCUE}

Who doesn't want to be rescued or liberated from those things in life that hold us hostage?

I know for myself, I wanted to be delivered because I had been held captive for far too long.

It wasn't until I found myself out of options. When I was at the "end of my rope!" That I became so desperate for God to rescue me, that I began to desire deliverance like never before.

I had heard about it, read about it, sang about it, and even hoped for it, but had I ever believed in it? The greater question was not that God could deliver me, but WOULD He deliver me?

Why is it that we believe God can and will do for everyone else, but we feel as though we don't deserve to have the same working miracle for our own life that He has done for so many others before?

Friend, if you are standing at the same place I was, can I encourage you to take the outstretched hand of Jesus and allow Him to set you free once and for all. None of us ever deserve it. He simply wants to do it for us.

He is *Deliverance!* That is what he came to earth for. That is His mission. To deliver us from sin, death and destruction of ourselves.

No matter what it is, and I mean no matter what, He wishes that you would be completely healed and set free.

David says it best in Psalm 3:8, *"From the Lord comes deliverance. May your blessings be on your people."*

Our friend David knows what it's like to be bound so tightly he can hardly breathe. His enemies were breathing down his neck. He had blown it badly with adultery and murder, that he's not sure if God will ever use him again. He made mistake after mistake, yet he knows God is the only one to deliver him. He knows he is his only saving grace.

As a matter of fact, you have to read what he says in Psalms 3. Now, I don't know about you, but I find it hard to demand anything from God, especially when I don't deserve it. But listen to David in verse 7, *Arise O LORD! Rescue me, O my God...* Wow! He is pretty bold telling God to get up and come to him. You also have to know something about the word LORD here. This is Yahweh. The Almighty. His name means the Great I Am. When you see all the letters capitalized in His name, this is all being, all knowing, all authority. This *THE LORD!*

But it also means Adonai which translates to "my LORD". And David knew just that. That God was his LORD. It was a very personal relationship, despite all he had done wrong.

I am not sure if I have ever demanded something from THE LORD like this ever. But David wasted no time in doing it.

I may have cried, begged, bargained and manipulated, but never demanded for God to deliver me from anywhere. Honestly, it kind of scares me to talk to God like this. However, this is also why we read that David was a friend to God and the apple of His eye. They were close despite his sinfulness.

David had committed premeditated murdered. He committed adultery, deceived and tried to cover it all up. But here is the part that gets me everytime. He knew that if he ever had a chance of getting out of this situation alive, it was going to take God Almighty to do it. He called on his LORD. And we can do the same without reservation.

So, where does that leave you? Afraid to come to the Throne Room boldly? Sheepish in your conversation with the Lord Almighty? Feeling alone, as though you have received what you deserved? I know, me too.

However, I do want to live free. Free from everything and anything that binds me. I do need rescued and I do need to be delivered, not only from the things of this world, but from myself.

So, I think we should start there. Right where David did, "LORD deliver me!" And that my friend is where you will see the LORD like you have never seen Him before.

As the song goes, He is for you, not against you! You're welcome to sing along. But first, I think I just heard a ding on your phone... you have a *delivery*! Go and be free!

ROCK CLIMBING Verses:

Psalm 32:7

You are my hiding place; you will protect me from trouble and surround me with songs of deliverance.

Psalm 34:4

I sought the LORD, and he answered me; he delivered me from all my fears.

Psalm 34:17

*The righteous cry out, and the L*ORD *hears them, he delivers them from all their troubles.*

Psalm 107:6

When our ancestors were in Egypt, they gave no thought to your miracles; they did not remember your many kindnesses, and they rebelled by the sea, the Red Sea.

Romans 8:1-10

Therefore, there is now no condemnation for those who are in Christ Jesus, because through Christ Jesus the law of the Spirit who gives life has set you[a] free from the law of sin and death. For what the law was powerless to do because it was weakened by the flesh, God did by sending his own Son in the likeness of sinful flesh to be a sin offering.[c] And so he condemned sin in the flesh, in order that the righteous requirement of the law might be fully met in us, who do not live according to the flesh but according to the Spirit.

Those who live according to the flesh have their minds set on what the flesh desires; but those who live in accordance with the Spirit have their minds set on what the Spirit desires. The mind governed by the flesh is death, but the mind governed by the Spirit is life and peace. The mind governed by the flesh is hostile to God; it does not submit to God's law, nor can it do so. Those who are in the realm of the flesh cannot please God. You, however, are not in the realm of the flesh but are in the realm of the Spirit, if indeed the Spirit of God lives in you. And if anyone does not have the Spirit of Christ, they do not belong to Christ. But if Christ is in you, then even though your body is subject to death because of sin, the Spirit gives life because of righteousness.

DEFEAT IS NOT AN OPTION

2 Corinthians 4:8-9

"We are hard pressed on every side, but not crushed; perplexed, but not abandoned; struck down, but not destroyed."

My heart is pounding harder than ever this time as I walk up the same hill that I do every day of my power walking routine. The hills' incline is so intense that by the time you crest the top you feel as if you have just run an all-out sprint down the track like you did back in the glory days of your high school career.

Short of being 25 years older and having a whole lot more aches and pains that streak through my body, my chest still feels the same and my gasping for air is no different. You know the pain that makes you feel as though your lungs are bleeding from the inside out. Your arms work desperately to pull you up the ascent, while your legs thrust through lunge after burning lunge to drive your body to the next level. Triumph is short lived because the next descending hill only transports you to the next painstaking rise of another. It is a love hate relationship I have with those hills. The truth of the matter is that I love to hate them. But I love the workout they give me in return. The kind where you can feel every sinful bite of caloric intake falling off your thighs while mastering this beast of a terrain.

Many of my friends and family have tried to walk this small tract of land with me, but very few make it for a second or third lap. They always seem to be ready to quit just after one short round of intense hiking. (Which I might add is only 15 minutes)

Regardless, I have used this passionate time of exercise as one of those most painful periods where it is just Jesus and me, (and the buzzards that are perched in the trees above) to duke out some of the hardest and most thought provoking questions I have for Him .

I had recently come out of a desert experience that has lasted more than 7 weeks. It was a time of heartache, frustration and confusion. An era of confession and cleansing, which I might add was extremely painful.

I repeatedly felt like Job and asked the same questions that he did to God. I probed with the one question when all is lost and you really don't care what the answer is. And that is, "why was I born anyway? When so much is wrong, and defeat is imminent. Why does any of this matter?

I can remember when those very words came to the surface of my lips. What in the world are you doing? Why is all this happening? Why did you create me anyways?

I can remember thinking….."Jesus, please come back and put me out of my misery!!!" But that was not the answer I got that day, and unfortunately He has not returned yet to take us home to be in glory. So I had to learn to live in a better state than I was in.

The answer I received that day was far from what my pitiful self-wanted to hear. It was when I crest that infamous hill that lay outside my front lawn, that I heard that still small booming voice, which cannot be discounted in any way shape or form. It was straight from heaven and this time it was loud! It was louder than my heart was beating and stronger than my lungs were pounding. God boldly said, "Defeat is not an option!" He knew I was nearing the end of my rope. I was giving up. I had nothing else to prove and quite honestly, I could care less about anything or anybody.

The Lords testing had come and gone day in and day out. And sometimes it seemed as if the tests were given hour by hour. I was feeling the penetrating desire to throw in the towel. To give up on my family, my marriage, my job, and even myself. I had had enough!!! And with not one ounce of relief in sight, my only thought was to cash it all in and say, "I am finished!"

I remember, after one particular test during this time frame, I texted both my husband and best friend and said, "I QUIT!" It was shortly after those notorious words, God put me on that hill for his last two cents on the matter. Funny how you think you have it all figured out when God shows up and lets you know that you don't have a clue what is going on.

I wanted to quit so badly I could taste it. All I wanted was out. I was tired of being everything for everybody. Watching others live selfishly, I was ready to have my number pulled for "it's my time now"

It didn't matter where I went or what I wanted to do, I just wanted to be anywhere but here. This my friend is a very dangerous place to be. If the opportunity presents itself while you are in a vulnerable position such as this, things can go extremely wrong, extremely fast. Be careful. Remember

Satan roams around like a lion seeking whom he can devour. (I Peter 5:8). He preys upon the weak, the wounded, the one isolated. I was certainly weak at this point in time and he knew it would be an opportune time to strike while I was down. But thankfully God had another plan for me. And He has one for you too.

Dr. Charles Stanley cautions us about these moments in time and uses the acronym HALT= HUNGRY-ANGRY-LONELY-TIRED. It is great advice to be on high alert when you are experiencing any or all of those symptoms in life. This is never a time to make a decision. Especially a life altering decision.

"Look up!!" were the words that I heard that day!. Look up and see that I am doing a new thing. Isaiah 43.

Often we are so connected with our media devices that we miss all the great things God is doing right in the midst of our storm. Just think how many times a day you look down to do something. Be it that at work, home or school. We are far too consumed with what is at hand. Rarely lifting our eyes unto the heavens where we should never look away from.

For a quick reality check, take an inventory sometime this week for an entire day on what you are focusing on. Now, I know most of our day is consumed with our occupation, but even with that we have seconds and sometimes moments when we can simply look up, look out, look around and whisper the words, "where are you Lord?" What are you doing today?" I would love to catch a glimpse of you, if even for a moment in time."

.

I can promise you this, if you take the time out of your schedule, God will take the time out of His, to delight you with His presence. The Word says that He dances over us. Can you imagine someone dancing over you because they are so in love with you? I can hardly fathom that expression no matter how hard I try. But it is true! Read it for yourself...Zephaniah 3:17

"Your GOD is present among you, a strong Warrior there to save you. Happy to have you back, he'll calm you with his love and delight you with his songs."

I know for some, you are in a restless season of life. Maybe you have been unemployed for far too long and you were wishing that God would dance Himself right over to your house and present you with a new career opportunity in the near future to save your home from being foreclosed on. Or maybe you are a student heading off to college on a scholarship as an athlete and you have your entire life plan set before you. Unfortunately, your other knee just blew out before the season even began dashing all your hopes and dreams. You're not really seeing God dance over you there either. Or the hopes of your 35 year marriage are long gone with the love of your life. It doesn't really matter about the scenario, you can fill in your own story here. All that matters is the emptiness you feel and hopelessness that is ever present with each breath you take.

Isaiah writes, "Look up! God commands, for I am doing a new thing". Is the "new thing" your way of doing it? Probably not, but we have to believe that we serve a sovereign God who is all knowing and who knows what's best for us. Friend, God is in the business of redemption. And just when you think all is lost, God often shows up in His finest moments.

There are two very fascinating stories in the bible where Jesus teaches his disciples about faith and trusting Him in uncertain times. The first is when the disciples were in the boat and the storm came upon them in the Sea of Galilee while Jesus was fast asleep. The disciples cried out not once, but twice, "Master, Master!" and then Jesus appeared to them peacefully from the stern of the boat. We know that this was not just any storm on the seas that evening. This storm was a squall. Have you ever watched the movie, "The Perfect Storm?" The same happens here. The lay of the land that envelopes the Sea of Galilee is optimum for the wind to come up from the underside causing great waves to toss the boats like little dinghies. They are beaten by gale force winds and terror has set in. It was the perfect storm.

I don't know about you, but a squall and a thunderstorm are two very different things. I always used to think this was just a quick storm that popped up on the sea. No sir! It was something out of control. Maybe like some of your lives feel right now. And the other interesting part of this story is that the bible says that God was *not* in this storm.

Now, we all know who calls the rain and the clouds, and even who casts the rays of sunshine for the rainbow to appear after the storm. But this particular storm was not of God. We know this because He rebuked the wind and said to the sea, "Hush now!" Be still (muzzled) Mark 4:39 (Amp. Bible). Did he ultimately let it pass their way? Absolutely! Was it used to show how little faith they had even with Jesus in the boat? Yes! Just think with Jesus physically in the confounds of this vessel, they still were scared to death.

How often do we allow our fear to overtake us when we know that Jesus is right there in the room with us? What storm is brewing amongst you and your family that brings waves over the sides of your life? Making you feel as though you will be washed away with one more blow to your already seemingly battered existence.

The second story is just as fascinating, but the scenario is a bit different. Jesus has been alone for many hours after a full day of teaching and miracles. The disciples get into another boat to go to the other side to get away from the crowds. It was somewhere between 3-6 o'clock in the morning and they were several miles out to sea when a storm of hurricane portions came upon this boat. Again, the bible says that the winds were against them. Jesus is never against us. Once more Jesus shows who is actually in control as he asks Peter to come to him even while the storm is still enraged. Jesus didn't call Peter after the storm had passed by. He called him right in the midst of its rage. How often does Jesus call us to come out of our most fear filled moments and to take His hand and trust him fully?

When we think of Peter, we often associate him with walking on water! How many times are you in the storm of your life and God calls out and says, "come to me, trust me, look up…keep your eyes on me!"

It is inevitably when we look down, we lose sight of our Father and we begin to sink. Jesus is saying to Peter as He is walking to Him on the water, waves splashing against him, "Look up Peter, keep your eyes on me. Defeat is not an option here. I am not going to let you sink to the bottom of this ocean." And neither, will God let you sink to the bottom of your ocean if you will just keep your eyes on Him.

As I finish this chapter many months later, I am excited to tell you that I have been redeemed from that very dark desert place I spoke about earlier. I recently met with a great author friend of mine who always tells me like it is. She said, "Shannon, you reek of redemption!" At first, I was taken back by such strong language. I really wasn't sure what to think. Was this a compliment or an insult?

As I traveled home that afternoon, I realized reeking wasn't such a bad thing. Think about it. When you have been redeemed by Christ, you should come away smelling and looking totally different. The fragrance of Jesus will always cast an amazing aroma. I guess she smelt or saw that on me. I bet Peter reeked of ocean water and the fish of the sea before the dawn began to rise that following morning. But I bet more than anything he too was a different man when he stepped back on the boat with the disciples from a wave, not from a plank or a dock. He would never be the same again. And neither was I. And neither will you be.

Although, I never would wish a desert experience on anyone. I would have to say, the outcome is so sweet on the other side.

I cannot describe the lonely hours and days that went by, but I know that as long as I kept my eyes on Jesus, defeat was never an option!

My prayer for you is, that whatever season you are going through at this very moment in time, you will begin to look up and immediately see the glory of the Lord shining upon your face. Feel the warmth of His embrace. And that you too will reek of redemption and never know the sights and sounds of defeat. Because it is never an option with God! Hang in there, your victory lap is just around the corner.

Rock Climbing Guide:

What is your greatest obstacle at this moment in time? Your health, your finances, your relationships, or your employment? You name it! Where do you feel most defeated? Your emotions, your self-image, your self-worth? Please know that you were created for a reason. And that God has amazing plans for your life right now and in the future, no matter how dark your current situation may seem.

Jeremiah 29:11-13 *"For I know the plans I have for you," declares the LORD, "plans to prosper you and not to harm you, plans to give you hope and a future. Then you will call on me and come and pray to me, and I will listen to you. You will seek me and find me when you seek me with all your heart."*

God often uses our greatest struggles to be our most defining moments so that He can receive the glory, but also so you can see Him for who He truly is….. your EVERYTHING! Look up friends. Look out, God is doing a new thing in your life today. I can't wait to hear all about it!!!

> Isaiah 43 : *1-But now, this is what the LORD says— he who created you, Jacob (fill your name in here), he who formed you, Israel: "Do not fear, for I have redeemed you;*
> *I have summoned you by name; you are mine. When you pass through the waters,*
> *I will be with you; and when you pass through the rivers, they will not sweep over you. When you walk through the fire, you will not be burned; the flames will not set you ablaze. For I am the LORD your God, the Holy One of*

Israel, your Savior; I give Egypt for your ransom,
Cush and Seba in your stead. Since you are precious and
honored in my sight, and because I love you, I will give
people in exchange for you, nations in exchange for your
life. Do not be afraid, for I am with you; I will bring your
children from the east and gather you from the west. I will
say to the north, 'Give them up!' and to the south, 'Do not
hold them back.'Bring my sons from afar and my daughters
from the ends of the earth—everyone who is called by my
name, whom I created for my glory, whom I formed and
made." lead out those who have eyes but are blind, who
have ears but are deaf. All the nations gather together and
the peoples assemble.
Which of their gods foretold this and proclaimed to us the
former things? Let them bring in their witnesses to prove
they were right, so that others may hear and say, "It is
true." "You are my witnesses," declares the LORD,
"and my servant whom I have chosen, so that you may
know and believe me and understand that I am he. Before
me no god was formed, nor will there be one after me. I,
even I, am the LORD, and apart from me there is no savior.
I have revealed and saved and proclaimed— I, and not
some foreign god among you. You are my witnesses,"
declares the LORD, "that I am God. Yes, and from ancient
days I am he. No one can deliver out of my hand.
When I act, who can reverse it?" This is what the LORD
says— your Redeemer, the Holy One of Israel: "For your
sake I will send to Babylon and bring down as fugitives all
the Babylonians, in the ships in which they took pride. I am
the LORD, your Holy One, Israel's Creator, your King."
This is what the LORD says— he who made a way through
the sea, path through the mighty waters, who drew out the

chariots and horses, the army and reinforcements together,
and they lay there, never to rise again, extinguished,
snuffed out like a wick: "Forget the former things; do not
*dwell on the past. **See, I am doing a new thing! Now it***
springs up; do you not perceive it?
I am making a way in the wilderness and streams in the
wasteland.

Friend, do you see it? God is doing a new thing. Hang on,
Your defeat is not an option! God is on the way.

Climbing Out From the Wreckage

It was a hot August day, when the temperature rose into the 90's. The afternoon sun was blazing hot on my skin. I was covered with a reddish brown tan, and my bright yellow shirt was a great compliment to the hard work of landscaping in the summer sun. I was scorched and tired and more than ready to end a tough day's work of edging, mulching and primping beds for a corporate building that stood for excellence in everything they did. The outside of the building must have an award winning look to accompany their alter ego image that preceded them everywhere they went. This was the approach to a multi-million dollar business. So, doing my job for this particular company not only came with great stress of perfection, but it needed to be done in a timely manner. Get in and get out! Leave nothing unturned. Bushes manicured, weeds removed, flowers planted and in bloom, edging precise, and mulch laid in the exact amount that would be the ultimate topping to any picture perfect landscape that would be fit for any exclusive garden magazine.

I remember this day like it was yesterday. The time was just after 3:00 pm on a Friday afternoon, and we were in the final haul for clearing the debris, and fine tuning the mulch in which we had labored for hours. There was a great sense of accomplishment, but the day was far from over unbeknownst to me.

Completing the day, I drove out of the corporate parking lot on my all-terrain vehicle (better known as a John Deere Gator), and stayed close to the curb as cars were traveling home from their own hard day and the end of their work week. As I approached the entrance and turned the corner to exit, I can remember this excruciating pain on the back of my head. I grabbed the left side and screamed, "Oh my gosh!!!!!!!!!!!" The next thing I knew I was lying in the grass up on the curb and feeling this intense burning on my right shoulder and leg. Where just a few moments ago, they felt a little crisp from the sun's rays. I was now feeling as though someone had an electric heat lamp on an open wound and it was burning my raw flesh. It wasn't a heat lamp, it was the blazing August sun from the road rash that now covered my body.

As I pulled out of the corporate driveway, an approaching truck came from behind and side swiped the John Deere gator while I was driving along the curb. The woman driving the vehicle had come from a neighboring trucking company and she was high tailing it out for the weekend. The passenger mirror collided with the left side of my head, which ultimately was torn off.

I now lay in excruciating pain, crying and bleeding, while another worker ran for help. I began contemplating while flat on my back, looking into the fiery hot sky, what would become of my life now. My left knee was throbbing where the tire of the truck pinned it to the steering wheel of my vehicle. The driver drove up onto the floor board subsequently first smashing my knee and then throwing me over the hood of the truck, catapulting me beside the mangled all-terrain vehicle. This is where I laid and waited for help which seemed like a lifetime. I listened with great anticipation as the sirens grew louder and closer. I thought, they are really coming for me aren't they?! Thank God someone was coming to my rescue. It is a glorious sound and frightening all at the same time when you are in this kind of pain. I think it only took a few minutes for the paramedics to arrive but it seemed like an hours.

I can remember one particular fireman that was gracious enough to hold his smoke-covered yellow coat high over my body, to block the penetrating sun rays that felt like razor blades cutting into my skin. He knew the pain I was in, when I cried, "the sun hurts so bad!"

As they assessed my injuries, and the state I was in,

they loaded me into the squad as quickly as possible and gave relief as much as they could. I hurt everywhere. My left side had just made contact with a speeding 3000 lb. metal pick up truck. My right side was shredded from the asphalt and my lower back had heat permeating that I would later learn was yet another injury. Something no one saw coming.

It was later that evening after all of the tests were done, and I was admitted into the hospital for observation, that I continued to smell gasoline. I lay in a hospital gown after they had washed my wounds and accessed my skin, that I could not get the smell of gas away from me. The nurse had removed all of my clothing earlier in the day, but I still had my underwear on and I had laid in a puddle of gasoline why the paramedics worked on me in the grass. It was now 9:00 p.m. in the evening. I had been laying with the gas directly on my lower back side the entire time. It slowly began burning my skin. When we realized what had happened it was too late. The gas had done its damage and the 2nd degree burn had begun to set in.

I could not lay on my right side, nor my left due to my injuries. And with each passing hour my lower back became more and more painful. I felt helpless. I was now out from the wreckage, but what was I to do? I could barely move. The aftermath from the accident was evident. I felt utter and complete helplessness!

Whether you feel as if you too are still under your own wreckage or you have just been pulled out to safety, the remnants are still there. The mangled metal and glass may not even be removed from your body or the street yet, but the extreme pain has set in. You can hear the people talking around you and possibly hear the sirens, but you now have a long way to go back to recovery. Maybe instead of glass and metal, it is the death notice of your child. Or possibly, the divorce papers from your spouse. Your wreckage may be that accident that killed your loved one, or the huge mess of financial chaos that threatens to leave you homeless. Whatever your wreckage looks like, no matter how large or small, it is painful to look at, and it is even more painful to see what damage it has done to you personally.

It took several weeks for my body to heal itself. I had to spend a lot of lonely days and nights watching my family carry on with their lives, while I was confined to my bed and sofa. I became irritable and depressed because this terrible wreck had taken part of my life from me. My great everyday life that we mothers love to hate became something of the past. We are women and we should be well enough to take care of everyone all of the time no matter what life throws our way. That was really hard for me. I was no longer "super mom". I was now a cripple, lying helpless on the sofa and found that getting up to go to the restroom was the biggest accomplishment of my day.

As I look back now, I can see where God was not only there that dreadfully hot day, but He was there in my loneliest hours while I recovered in the weeks that followed.

During one of the darkest days, my dearest friend Cheryl had brought me a book and said, "I am not sure why I am supposed to give this to you but here it is"

The book was, "Just Enough Light For The Step I Am On" by Stormie Omartian. It was God's love letter to me in the days and weeks to come. I read through it so fast that I reread it again a few days later.

I was seeing God in a whole new light. Literally. This was a divine appointment. I know people struggle with the thought that a loving Father allows such terrible things to happen to His children, but I truly believe He did.

I was slowly killing myself each day running my business. I had shoved God out of the way to do my own thing and pursue my own ideas and agendas. And it cost me greatly.

I thought I knew best and it still brings tears to my eyes of what truly could have happened to my family if God had not spared my life that day. God was so gracious every step of the way. This was not the first nor the last time that He would save my life when I could easily have been killed.

I am sure that there are many that read this that may not have been spared this outcome. But I do believe with all of my heart that if you will allow God to pick you up and out of the wreckage that you will be better for it in the long run. He will do a great and mighty work in your life, if you will allow Him to rescue you.

Just as I could not physically get up and put myself in that ambulance, you too may not be able to pick yourself up and go for help. You may need to call the ultimate 911 operator and listen for the sirens. I promise they are coming for you. God promises to answer your cries. If you are not certain, return to the chapter "Cry's from the Canyon" for more reading.

God had me exactly where He wanted me. I unfortunately did not want to be pinned down to the sofa, but I tend to be hard headed and God had tried to get my attention on numerous occasions. I hate to admit it, but I ignored His warnings because I wanted things my way.

God spoke volumes to me the week that I was incapacitated. I saw Him in a fresh new light and I needed to stop and take notice of what it was that He was trying to tell me.

He wanted to show me that He is enough. Period!!! That I did not need to go and fill my life with hopeless things of today that would never fulfill me in my tomorrows.

God often only gives us enough light for the step that we are on because we can only handle that amount at that moment in time.

If we see too far into the future, we often take it upon ourselves to get there the quickest way possible, missing all that God has in store to teach us along the way. Rarely, do we stop, wait and listen for more instructions. When we don't we quickly start out again, and we end right back in our original debris. And then the process starts all over again.

So, what wreckage are you paralyzed by? What damage has been done to your mind, body and soul? Would you be honest with yourself and allow the Lord to come and rescue you from it all? Or will you continue to go at mach speed until even greater damage is done? The choice is yours. Either we stop before it's too late or God will stop us before something worse happens. Remember, He loves us too much to leave us the way we are. But that my friend is up to you…

Survival Guide Notes

What does your wreckage look like? Can you breathe? Can you see anything? Is anyone coming for help? Do you hear the sirens getting closer? Are you bleeding? Are your bones bruised or broken? Or is it your spirit that has taken the blow? Have you been crippled in your walk with the Lord? Do you even have a Savior that you call Lord? Someone must heal you from your brokenness. Someone must bandage your wounds. They will need to pick you up out of the wreckage and take you to safety. The Lord is waiting. He stands over your wreckage. He knows every piece that has been damaged and yet He knows what He can salvage. Allow Him today to take you by the hand, to carry you out of harm's way and take you to the ultimate place of healing. Into His arms...

I can't tell you that there won't be days of pain. I felt much worse before I ever got better. But please believe me (someone that has been there) that He does work it all out for you good. (Romans 8:28)

And ultimately for his glory. In the book "Brokenness" by Nancy Leigh DeMoss, she states that true brokenness must come before God moves in a mighty way in your life. If you are broken from the wreckage, rejoice, because God is about to do a miracle in your life.

Survival Guide Verses

Psalm 31:23

Be brave. Be strong. Don't give up. Expect God to get here soon.

Psalm 31 :5 *I've put my life in your hands. You won't drop me, you'll never let me down.*

Psalm 34:18-20

If your heart is broken, you'll find God right there; if you're kicked in the gut, he'll help you catch your breath. Disciples so often get into trouble; still, God is there every time. He's your bodyguard, shielding every bone; not even a finger gets broken.

Psalm 33:18-19 *Watch this: God's eye is on those who respect him, the ones who are looking for his love. He's ready to come to their rescue in bad times; in lean times he keeps body and soul together.*

Psalm 34:6 *When I was desperate, I called out, and God got me out of a tight spot.*

Psalm 34: 17 *Is anyone crying for help? God is listening, ready to rescue you*

HEALING

"Jesus wants to heal you everywhere you hurt"
Psalm 147:3 He heals the brokenhearted and binds up their
wounds.

Healing is one of the most beautiful words known to mankind.
Ask anyone if they want to be healed from something and
99.9% of people would say, "Yes!"
In the year 2023, there is certainly no lack of medicinal
healing. Big Pharma has made sure that none of us go
without when it comes to the medicines we need to make us
feel better. Whether that is a quick fix or long term care, there
is a pill for it. But with that knowledge, it makes me wonder
why so many are still sick and suffering, especially in
America where pharmaceuticals flow like the turning on of
the faucet in our kitchen sinks.

With a trillion dollar industry, it's hard to believe that
any of us would stay sick or be in need of healing for very
long. However, statistically we are more sick than ever. Not
only physically, but mentally, emotionally and spiritually.
The art of healing goes back to the beginning of time. God
has never left us to fend for ourselves or for us to suffer alone
when it comes to our infirmities. Not only does God heal us

as the scripture reads in Psalm 147:3, but he says that he will come near to us when we are sick and hurting.

When was the last time you needed God to heal from sickness or something that was broken? Maybe it was your kidney or lung. Possibly a leg or an arm or even your heart. Jesus is in the business of healing, and he wants to heal you everywhere you hurt.

There was a man who had laid at the Pool of Bethesda for 38 years. He was an invalid with no way to heal himself, nor take himself to anyone who could. However, for whatever reason Jesus decided to pass underneath the colonnade on that particular day, at that particular time, to meet this man for a particular time of healing.

Had he done something to deserve The Almighty to look his way, or pass by his mat? We don't know, because the bible does not reveal in any way that this man deserved to be healed. He was simply like every other person lying next to the healing pool that day.

We get very little insight to this man's conditions other than he has laid desperately trying to get into the waters that healed. All we know is that every time he made his way in, someone else took his place in line to receive healing.

Many of us are lying in hopes of God's healing, but have suffered for years with great sadness, when God didn't heal us?

Neither you nor I will ever know why God chooses to heal some and not others while we live on earth. However, I do know that I have lived long enough to see that God is still in the healing business. And that he is still performing miracles.

Although I often question why and why not God, I know those answers may never come until I get to heaven. If you're breathing, you may always wonder why God heals one and not the other. Or does He? Just because we don't see His healing here on earth, does that mean he does not answer our desperate prayers?

No prayers are left unheard and/or unanswered. Sometimes, He says, Yes! Sometimes, it's No! And sometimes the answer is wait! And that can be the hardest one of all.

If your loved one has cancer and you pray fervently for them to be healed and God does not heal them here on earth, does that mean he didn't answer your prayers? I don't believe so.

God may very well choose to heal your loved one on the other side of glory and make them completely whole. We are just saddened because we don't get to see that healing here on earth in front of us.

If God does not heal your marriage, does that mean He does not care about your family or your well being? No! He loves you way too much to not heal you.
However, your healing may come in a completely different form than you ever thought possible.

What if your healing comes through your tears or through prayers? What if your healing comes through all the heartache and pain? What if your healing comes through caring for someone who didn't lose their loved one but you are now bringing help in healing through your own loss? God will use whatever means necessary to heal you at the deepest level.

Remember the man at the pool of Bethesda? Jesus told him to pick up his mat and go so that he doesn't fall back into sin *again*. This verse got me thinking. Had he sinned to get himself into this situation? We don't know. But if it is in the bible then there is a reason. Maybe he did nothing wrong like those who question why the young boy was blind. Was it because he had done something wrong or his parents?
No, it's just the way he was, but either way, Jesus can and will heal you. All you have to do is cry out to him. Look for him, or watch to see when he passes by.

Yes, God has given us all the great gifts of modern medicine, but when was the last time you called on the great Physician to heal you? To heal you in the places that no one can see. In the place that not even the most technologically advanced machine can see.

Jesus' eye is on you and your pain beloved. He wishes that no one will perish. But that doesn't mean that we will live forever. No that means he wishes no one will perish without Him.

Jesus knows better than anyone that we live in a sin sick world and that we will suffer from the ravages of this dying planet. However, He does not leave us to care for ourselves. Matthew 11:28 reminds us, *"Come to me, all you who are weary and burdened and I will give you rest."*

First and foremost, we must come to Him. Secondly, we read in Jeremiah 33:6 *"Behold, I will bring it health and cure them and will reveal unto them the abundance of peace and truth"*.

God is wanting to heal you not only in one area of your life but everywhere you hurt.

Would you allow the great Physician to begin to apply his healing balm to your soul? Let the Lord Almighty search your mind, body and soul to begin your regime of healing. He will truly make you whole!

The Rescue Mission

   I know with all certainty what Satan meant for my harm, Jesus has turned for my good.
 I no longer can deny the *Rescue Mission* that Christ commissioned 2000 years ago has been in play nearly all of my life. He is my ***only*** hope! And He is your only hope too.
   From the beginning days of my life, I was destined for a pit that no one returns from let alone survives. Although I have been in church since my mothers womb, it has taken over a half of a century that Jesus has to come to rescue me from the greatest threat of all, MYSELF! He set out on a mission to rescue me, from me!
   As I have fallen into and lived in this pit of hell while being on earth, I have found that there is only one solution to all that threatens to destroy you and me. His name is JESUS.
   John 10:10 says, *"The thief comes only to steal, and kill and destroy; BUT I have come that they may have life, and have it to the full."*
   It wasn't until I wrote this scripture out for this chapter that I noticed the "ands". All of these years, I used to read or teach, that he came to "steal, kill and destroy." That is not accurate. It says he comes to steal AND kill AND destroy. Not just one of those horrible acts, but ALL of them. And he has done a bang up job in my life, and I am pretty certain if you are holding this book in your hands today that he has done the same to you.
   Well friend, I want to be the first to tell you that you are coming up and out of this God forsaken hole. The endless

nights of sleep with tear drenched sheets are coming to an end. The torment of anxiety and depression are going to be restored with hope and healing. The years that the locusts have stolen will be given back with a double portion. God is about to turn your mourning in gladness and your tears into rejoicing. This is the year of the Lord's favor.

Isaiah 61:1-4; & 7 "The Spirit of the Lord is on me, because the Lord has anointed me to preach good news to the poor. He has sent me to bind up the broken hearted, to proclaim freedom for the captives and release from darkness for the prisoners...to comfort all who mourn and provide for those who grieve in Zion- to bestow on them a crown of beauty instead of ashes, the oil of gladness instead of mourning and a garment of praise instead of a spirit of despair. They will be called oaks of righteousness, a planting of the Lord for the displaying of his splendor. They will rebuild the ancient ruins and restore the places long devastated, they will renew the ruined cities that have been devastated for generations." " Instead of their shame my people will receive a double portion, and instead of disgrace they will rejoice in their land and everlasting joy will be theirs"

I know where you are sitting right now, and all of that seems like a long lost dream. However, if it's in the bible then it's going to happen. That is a promise, and you can take that to Heavens bank. If one promise is false, then all of them are false. God is not a God that he can lie. And His promise doesn't rely on you. They are His and His alone. His name is Faithful and TRUE!

I have personally felt and experienced this "Rescue Mission". I know what deep sadness and suffering feels like, along with great gladness and rejoicing. Not the kind of experience the world offers, but the kind that only Jesus Christ can offer.

Remember the second half of John 10:10? Oftentimes we stop at the comma, amd put more emphasis on what Satan is doing then what Jesus is doing. You must read on and claim this promise as your own. It says that He (Jesus) comes that you may life and have it abundantly. To the fullest extent! That means God wants His best for you.

I don't know about you, but I struggle with all the wrong I have done in my life that God would ever do this for me. But if I ever hope to get out of this place alive, I realize I have to start believing in God's word for myself if I ever want to see victory.

There is a particular passage in the bible that leaves me speechless every time I read it. But I would leave you uninformed if I left it out of this book. It's a passage that continually takes my breath away, but it also fills my heart with utter joy that God could love me this much and wants nothing but the best for me. Take it in for yourself!

Zephaniah 3:14-20 " Sing O Daughter, O Son! Shout aloud! Be glad and rejoice with all your heart. The LORD has taken away your punishment, he has turned back your enemy. The LORD, the King of Israel, is with you, never again will you fear any harm. On that day, they will say to Jerusalem, Do not let your hands hang limp. The LORD your God is with you, he is mighty to save. He will take great delight in you, he will quiet you with his love, he will rejoice over with singing.

The sorrows for the appointed feasts I will remove from you;
they are a burden and a reproach to you. At that time I will
deal with all who oppressed you; I will rescue the lame and
gather those who have been scattered. I will give them praise
and honor in every land where they were put to shame. At that
time I will gather you; at that time I will bring you home, I
will give you honor and praise among all the peoples of the
earth when I restore your fortunes before your very eyes, says
the LORD."

This my friend, is one of the greatest promises in the bible for you and me. I know I don't deserve for the LORD to rejoice over me, let alone restore everything I have done to destroy my own life, but he says He will restore it back to me. And He will do the same for you. The only thing I see in the passage for us to do is to sing and sing loud. Not in our current circumstances, but to rejoice that we are being rescued. Help is coming for you, friend. You will be taken from this pit of despair and be made whole again.

For years I had asked the LORD to deliver me from my past, my mistakes, my pain, my guilt and shame. That was my constant prayer. But with these petitions, it also became my rescue cry. The *Rescue Mission* that came from the heart of heaven became the rescue from the greatest enemy of all, me! Never did I realize that I needed to be delivered from the very thing that was destroying my life. My entire life was all about me.

In a day and age where "I" precedes all of our devices such as "I-Phone", "I-Watch" "I-pad" and of course the ultimate self indulgence, "Selfie", life can't be anything but about me. And that is exactly what the enemy wants you and I to do. Make yourself god so that you won't worship the GOD of the universe. Remember his mission is to kill and steal and destroy. Also remember, that that is the very reason he was expelled from heaven. PRIDE. Life was all about him, and in his eyes there wasn't room for anyone else, especially God. And with that mindset, he ultimately destroyed himself. Satan is a defeated foe. Revelation tells us, he was handed a fatal blow on the day Jesus proclaimed, "It is finished!" Now he is just bleeding out on his way down to his final destination. His personal mission is to take as many souls with him before God sentences him and locks him to his certain death for eternity.

As I write to you my afflicted friend, I want you to know that I too have traveled this arduous journey that you are facing and this is not the end. The Lord has allowed me to travel to the depths of despair to finally hit "Rock Bottom." At first, I found it as a curse upon my life and nothing short of cruelty. But God in His sovereignty has shown me that it is greater to have been rescued from destruction than to have been lost and never found.

This book is a snapshot of what it means to experience that dreadful place. At the same time, this experience is the most amazing rescue mission of all. Jesus is the Rescue Mission. He will be the one who reaches down and you will take His nail scarred hand and bring you to your solid footing again. You will be placed upon The Rock. Not just any rock.

The writer of Psalms pens it best in *Psalms 18:16-19, "He reached down from on high and took hold of me; he drew me out of deep waters. He rescued me from my powerful enemy, from my foes who were too strong for me. They confronted me in the day of my disaster, but the LORD was my support. HE brought me out into a spacious place; he rescued me because He delighted in me."*

And then the reassurance of Isaiah 59:1 " Surely the arm of the LORD is not too short to save, nor his ear too dull to hear.

Hurting friend, you are right where God can see you. You are not out of reach or off of His radar no matter what you have done or how far you have fallen.

For those who may not know Him yet, may I introduce you to the man who rescued me. He's my closest friend, His name is Jesus. He did not come to condemn, but to rescue you from this sin sick world. As long as we live in this land, we will experience trouble, but he promises to never leave us or forsake us in that place.

If you are unsure where to start or what to say, I'd like to introduce you to a passage in the bible that was most helpful to me when I was at my lowest point in life. I would encourage you to read this out loud as a prayer.

Did you know that all of heaven is harkened when they hear the Word of the LORD? Just know that He WILL hear your broken voice and He will come to your rescue. All you need to do is cry out.

Psalm 142 "I cry out loudly to GOD, loudly I plead with GOD for mercy. I spill out all my complaints before him, and spell out my troubles in detail. As I sink in despair, my spirit ebbing away, you know how I'm feeling, Know the danger I'm in, the traps hidden in my path. Look right, look left—there's not a soul who cares what

happens! I'm up against the wall, with no exit—it's just me, all alone. I cry out, GOD, call out: 'You're my last chance, my only hope for life!'
Oh listen, please listen; I've never been this low. Rescue me from those who are hunting me down; I'm no match for them. Get me out of this dungeon so I can thank you in public. Your people will form a circle around me and you'll bring me showers of blessing!"

Psalm 143 " Listen to this prayer of mine, GOD; pay attention to what I'm asking. Answer me—you're famous for your answers! Do what's right for me. But don't, please don't, haul me into court; not a person alive would be acquitted there. The enemy hunted me down; he kicked me and stomped me within an inch of my life. He put me in a black hole, buried me like a corpse in that dungeon. I sat there in despair, my spirit draining away, my heart heavy, like lead. I remembered the old days, went over all you've done, pondered the ways you've worked, Stretched out my hands to you, as thirsty for you as a desert thirst for rain. Hurry with your answer, GOD! I'm nearly at the end of my rope. Don't turn away; don't ignore me! That would be certain death. If you wake me each morning with the sound of your loving voice, I'll go to sleep each night trusting in you. Point out the road I must travel; I'm all ears, all eyes before you. Save me from my enemies, GOD— you're my only hope!
Teach me how to live to please you, because you're my God. Lead me by your blessed Spirit into cleared and level pastureland. Keep up your reputation, God—give me life! In your justice, get me out of this trouble!

In your great love, vanquish my enemies; make a clean sweep of those who harass me. And why? Because I'm your servant!

In conclusion; this may feel like the end of your life, your marriage, your health, your parenting, or your reputation, but I have been sent to tell you, this is not the end of your rope, you are simply invited to reach for a new rope. The Rope of Hope. God is waiting to meet you there.
I can't wait to meet you at the top!

If you need additional support emotionally, mentally or spiritually, please reach out to us at Journey Living Ministries. We are here to help get you to safety. **No one is too far gone.** Jesus came on a rescue mission from heaven to earth just for you.

Journeyliving.org   The SOZO Center

Galatians 1:3-4 " Grace and peace to you from God our Father and the LORD Jesus Christ, who gave himself for our sins to rescue us from the present evil age, according to the will of our God and Father.

SPECIAL NOTE:

I now dedicate this book in memory of the late Scott Maier. On 1.19.2024, my husband took his first breath in heaven just prior to the release of this book on 2.11.2024 which would have been our 35th wedding anniversary.
 He got to hold the final copy in his hands and began to read it just before the Lord healed him completely. I had the privilege to watch Jesus personally reach down and take him out of the depths of cancer and disease and set him free for eternity. Although he will be greatly missed, how could we ever be saddened by his new life in heaven. Live Free my love!
To God be the glory!